# Send Me a Message

## Alan Trussell-Cullen

Dominie Press, Inc.

Publisher:  Christine Yuen
Series Editors:  Adria F. Klein & Alan Trussell-Cullen
Editors:  Bob Rowland & Paige Sanderson
Illustrator:  David Preston Smith
Designers:  Gary Hamada & Lois Stanfield

Published by:

## ꝑ Dominie Press, Inc.

1949 Kellogg Avenue
Carlsbad, California 92008  USA

www.dominie.com

ISBN  0-7685-0580-1

Printed in Singapore by PH Productions Pte Ltd

1 2 3 4 5 6 PH 03 02 01

ITP

# Table of Contents

In the olden days, if you wanted to send someone a message, you had to get someone to take it to them.

What do we do today?
We still send messages this way.

Did you know...? Every year
the United States Postal Service
delivers over 100 million letters
and over one million parcels.

POM PUM POM

POM PUM POM

8

In the olden days, people sent messages to each other through the air. They sent smoke signals. They used drumbeats.

What do we do today?
We still send messages
through the air. We send
radio and television signals
through the air. We send
some telephone messages
through the air, too.

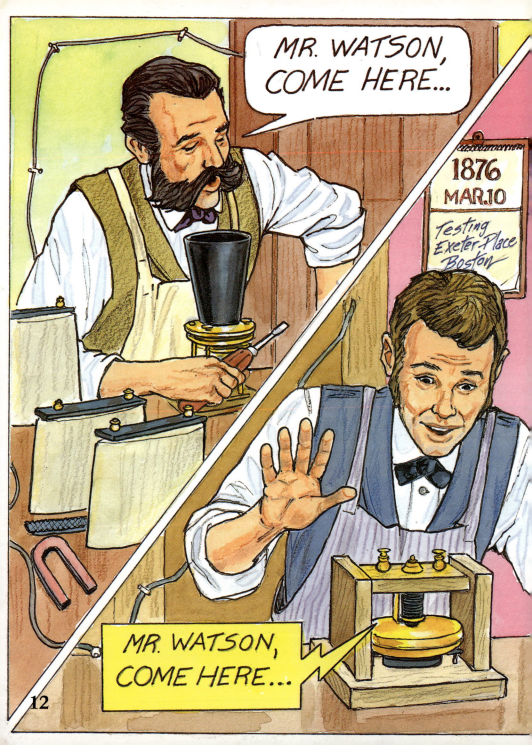

In 1876, Alexander Graham Bell sent a message along a wire to a person in the next room.

HI THERE
COMPUTER
XY249
HOW ARE YOU
FEELING TODAY?

NOT BAD
COMPUTER
JK239
HOW ABOUT YOU?

14

What do we do today?

We still send messages along wires.

People talk on telephones.

Computers send messages
to other computers.

Cable television comes to us
along a wire.

There is one way people have been sending messages for thousands of years, and it hasn't changed. Can you guess what it is?

We can tell people.

We can send it along a wire.

**How can we send a message today?**

We can write it down and mail it.

We can send it through the air.

# Picture Glossary

computer:

telephone:

radio:

television:

# Index